Password
Slut

Kay D Johnson

Johnson, Kay D
Password Slut

ISBN 978-1790479931 (pkb)

**Since this book holds all your
private and valuable information,
please keep this book in a
safe place at all times.**

Website:	**A**
Email:	
User Name:	
Password:	
Security Question/Hint	
Notes:	

Website:
Email:
User Name:
Password:
Security Question/Hint
Notes:

Website:
Email:
User Name:
Password:
Security Question/Hint
Notes:

A

Website:
Email:
User Name:
Password:
Security Question/Hint
Notes:

Website:
Email:
User Name:
Password:
Security Question/Hint
Notes:

Website:
Email:
User Name:
Password:
Security Question/Hint
Notes:

| Website: |
| Email: |
| User Name: |
| Password: |
| |
| |
| Security Question/Hint |
| |
| Notes: |
| |

A

| Website: |
| Email: |
| User Name: |
| Password: |
| |
| |
| Security Question/Hint |
| |
| Notes: |
| |

| Website: |
| Email: |
| User Name: |
| Password: |
| |
| |
| Security Question/Hint |
| |
| Notes: |
| |

A

Website:
Email:
User Name:
Password:
Security Question/Hint
Notes:

Website:
Email:
User Name:
Password:
Security Question/Hint
Notes:

User Name:
Password:
Security Question/Hint
Notes:

B

| Website: |
| Email: |
| User Name: |
| Password: |
| |
| |
| Security Question/Hint |
| |
| Notes: |
| |

| Website: |
| Email: |
| User Name: |
| Password: |
| |
| |
| Security Question/Hint |
| |
| Notes: |
| |

| Website: |
| Email: |
| User Name: |
| Password: |
| |
| |
| Security Question/Hint |
| |
| Notes: |
| |

B

Website:
Email:
User Name:
Password:
Security Question/Hint
Notes:

Website:
Email:
User Name:
Password:
Security Question/Hint
Notes:

Website:
Email:
User Name:
Password:
Security Question/Hint
Notes:

B

Website:
Email:
User Name:
Password:
Security Question/Hint
Notes:

Website:
Email:
User Name:
Password:
Security Question/Hint
Notes:

Website:
Email:
User Name:
Password:
Security Question/Hint
Notes:

B

Website:
Email:
User Name:
Password:
Security Question/Hint
Notes:

Website:
Email:
User Name:
Password:
Security Question/Hint
Notes:

Website:
Email:
User Name:
Password:
Security Question/Hint
Notes:

Website:
Email:
User Name:
Password:
Security Question/Hint
Notes:

C

Website:
Email:
User Name:
Password:
Security Question/Hint
Notes:

Website:
Email:
User Name:
Password:
Security Question/Hint
Notes:

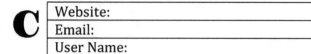

C

Website:
Email:
User Name:
Password:
Security Question/Hint
Notes:

Website:
Email:
User Name:
Password:
Security Question/Hint
Notes:

Website:
Email:
User Name:
Password:
Security Question/Hint
Notes:

C

Website:
Email:
User Name:
Password:
Security Question/Hint
Notes:

Website:
Email:
User Name:
Password:
Security Question/Hint
Notes:

Website:
Email:
User Name:
Password:
Security Question/Hint
Notes:

C

Website:
Email:
User Name:
Password:
Security Question/Hint
Notes:

Website:
Email:
User Name:
Password:
Security Question/Hint
Notes:

Website:
Email:
User Name:
Password:
Security Question/Hint
Notes:

D

| Website: |
| Email: |
| User Name: |
| Password: |
| |
| |
| Security Question/Hint |
| |
| Notes: |
| |

| Website: |
| Email: |
| User Name: |
| Password: |
| |
| |
| Security Question/Hint |
| |
| Notes: |
| |

| Website: |
| Email: |
| User Name: |
| Password: |
| |
| |
| Security Question/Hint |
| |
| Notes: |
| |

D

Website:	
Email:	
User Name:	
Password:	
Security Question/Hint	
Notes:	

Website:	
Email:	
User Name:	
Password:	
Security Question/Hint	
Notes:	

Website:	
Email:	
User Name:	
Password:	
Security Question/Hint	
Notes:	

D

Website:
Email:
User Name:
Password:
Security Question/Hint
Notes:

Website:
Email:
User Name:
Password:
Security Question/Hint
Notes:

Website:
Email:
User Name:
Password:
Security Question/Hint
Notes:

D

Website:
Email:
User Name:
Password:
Security Question/Hint
Notes:

Website:
Email:
User Name:
Password:
Security Question/Hint
Notes:

Website:
Email:
User Name:
Password:
Security Question/Hint
Notes:

E

Website:
Email:
User Name:
Password:
Security Question/Hint
Notes:

Website:
Email:
User Name:
Password:
Security Question/Hint
Notes:

Website:
Email:
User Name:
Password:
Security Question/Hint
Notes:

E

Website:
Email:
User Name:
Password:
Security Question/Hint
Notes:

Website:
Email:
User Name:
Password:
Security Question/Hint
Notes:

Website:
Email:
User Name:
Password:
Security Question/Hint
Notes:

E

Website:
Email:
User Name:
Password:
Security Question/Hint
Notes:

Website:
Email:
User Name:
Password:
Security Question/Hint
Notes:

Website:
Email:
User Name:
Password:
Security Question/Hint
Notes:

Website:
Email:
User Name:
Password:
Security Question/Hint
Notes:

Website:
Email:
User Name:
Password:
Security Question/Hint
Notes:

Website:
Email:
User Name:
Password:
Security Question/Hint
Notes:

F

| Website: |
| Email: |
| User Name: |
| Password: |
| |
| |
| Security Question/Hint |
| |
| Notes: |
| |

| Website: |
| Email: |
| User Name: |
| Password: |
| |
| |
| Security Question/Hint |
| |
| Notes: |
| |

| Website: |
| Email: |
| User Name: |
| Password: |
| |
| |
| Security Question/Hint |
| |
| Notes: |
| |

Website:
Email:
User Name:
Password:
Security Question/Hint
Notes:

Website:
Email:
User Name:
Password:
Security Question/Hint
Notes:

Website:
Email:
User Name:
Password:
Security Question/Hint
Notes:

F

| Website: |
| Email: |
| User Name: |
| Password: |
| |
| |
| Security Question/Hint |
| |
| Notes: |
| |

| Website: |
| Email: |
| User Name: |
| Password: |
| |
| |
| Security Question/Hint |
| |
| Notes: |
| |

| Website: |
| Email: |
| User Name: |
| Password: |
| |
| |
| Security Question/Hint |
| |
| Notes: |
| |

F

| Website: |
| Email: |
| User Name: |
| Password: |
| |
| |
| Security Question/Hint |
| |
| Notes: |
| |

| Website: |
| Email: |
| User Name: |
| Password: |
| |
| |
| Security Question/Hint |
| |
| Notes: |
| |

| Website: |
| Email: |
| User Name: |
| Password: |
| |
| |
| Security Question/Hint |
| |
| Notes: |
| |

G

Website:
Email:
User Name:
Password:
Security Question/Hint
Notes:

Website:
Email:
User Name:
Password:
Security Question/Hint
Notes:

Website:
Email:
User Name:
Password:
Security Question/Hint
Notes:

G

Website:
Email:
User Name:
Password:
Security Question/Hint
Notes:

Website:
Email:
User Name:
Password:
Security Question/Hint
Notes:

Website:
Email:
User Name:
Password:
Security Question/Hint
Notes:

G

Website:
Email:
User Name:
Password:
Security Question/Hint
Notes:

Website:
Email:
User Name:
Password:
Security Question/Hint
Notes:

Website:
Email:
User Name:
Password:
Security Question/Hint
Notes:

G

Website:
Email:
User Name:
Password:
Security Question/Hint
Notes:

Website:
Email:
User Name:
Password:
Security Question/Hint
Notes:

Website:
Email:
User Name:
Password:
Security Question/Hint
Notes:

H

| Website: |
| Email: |
| User Name: |
| Password: |
| |
| |
| Security Question/Hint |
| |
| Notes: |
| |

| Website: |
| Email: |
| User Name: |
| Password: |
| |
| |
| Security Question/Hint |
| |
| Notes: |
| |

| Website: |
| Email: |
| User Name: |
| Password: |
| |
| |
| Security Question/Hint |
| |
| Notes: |
| |

H

Website:
Email:
User Name:
Password:
Security Question/Hint
Notes:

Website:
Email:
User Name:
Password:
Security Question/Hint
Notes:

Website:
Email:
User Name:
Password:
Security Question/Hint
Notes:

H

Website:
Email:
User Name:
Password:
Security Question/Hint
Notes:

Website:
Email:
User Name:
Password:
Security Question/Hint
Notes:

Website:
Email:
User Name:
Password:
Security Question/Hint
Notes:

H

Website:
Email:
User Name:
Password:
Security Question/Hint
Notes:

Website:
Email:
User Name:
Password:
Security Question/Hint
Notes:

Website:
Email:
User Name:
Password:
Security Question/Hint
Notes:

Website:
Email:
User Name:
Password:
Security Question/Hint
Notes:

I

Website:
Email:
User Name:
Password:
Security Question/Hint
Notes:

Website:
Email:
User Name:
Password:
Security Question/Hint
Notes:

I

| Website: |
| Email: |
| User Name: |
| Password: |
| |
| |
| Security Question/Hint |
| |
| Notes: |
| |

| Website: |
| Email: |
| User Name: |
| Password: |
| |
| |
| Security Question/Hint |
| |
| Notes: |
| |

| Website: |
| Email: |
| User Name: |
| Password: |
| |
| |
| Security Question/Hint |
| |
| Notes: |
| |

I

Website:
Email:
User Name:
Password:
Security Question/Hint
Notes:

Website:
Email:
User Name:
Password:
Security Question/Hint
Notes:

Website:
Email:
User Name:
Password:
Security Question/Hint
Notes:

I

Website:
Email:
User Name:
Password:
Security Question/Hint
Notes:

Website:
Email:
User Name:
Password:
Security Question/Hint
Notes:

Website:
Email:
User Name:
Password:
Security Question/Hint
Notes:

J

Website:
Email:
User Name:
Password:
Security Question/Hint
Notes:

Website:
Email:
User Name:
Password:
Security Question/Hint
Notes:

Website:
Email:
User Name:
Password:
Security Question/Hint
Notes:

J

Website:
Email:
User Name:
Password:
Security Question/Hint
Notes:

Website:
Email:
User Name:
Password:
Security Question/Hint
Notes:

Website:
Email:
User Name:
Password:
Security Question/Hint
Notes:

J

Website:
Email:
User Name:
Password:
Security Question/Hint
Notes:

Website:
Email:
User Name:
Password:
Security Question/Hint
Notes:

Website:
Email:
User Name:
Password:
Security Question/Hint
Notes:

J

Website:
Email:
User Name:
Password:
Security Question/Hint
Notes:

Website:
Email:
User Name:
Password:
Security Question/Hint
Notes:

Website:
Email:
User Name:
Password:
Security Question/Hint
Notes:

K

Website:	
Email:	
User Name:	
Password:	
Security Question/Hint	
Notes:	

Website:
Email:
User Name:
Password:
Security Question/Hint
Notes:

Website:
Email:
User Name:
Password:
Security Question/Hint
Notes:

K

Website:
Email:
User Name:
Password:
Security Question/Hint
Notes:

Website:
Email:
User Name:
Password:
Security Question/Hint
Notes:

Website:
Email:
User Name:
Password:
Security Question/Hint
Notes:

K

Website:
Email:
User Name:
Password:
Security Question/Hint
Notes:

Website:
Email:
User Name:
Password:
Security Question/Hint
Notes:

Website:
Email:
User Name:
Password:
Security Question/Hint
Notes:

Website:

Email:

User Name:

Password:

Security Question/Hint

Notes:

Website:

Email:

User Name:

Password:

Security Question/Hint

Notes:

Website:

Email:

User Name:

Password:

Security Question/Hint

Notes:

Website:	**L**
Email:	
User Name:	
Password:	
Security Question/Hint	
Notes:	

Website:
Email:
User Name:
Password:
Security Question/Hint
Notes:

Website:
Email:
User Name:
Password:
Security Question/Hint
Notes:

L

Website:
Email:
User Name:
Password:
Security Question/Hint
Notes:

Website:
Email:
User Name:
Password:
Security Question/Hint
Notes:

Website:
Email:
User Name:
Password:
Security Question/Hint
Notes:

L

Website:
Email:
User Name:
Password:
Security Question/Hint
Notes:

Website:
Email:
User Name:
Password:
Security Question/Hint
Notes:

Website:
Email:
User Name:
Password:
Security Question/Hint
Notes:

L

Website:
Email:
User Name:
Password:
Security Question/Hint
Notes:

Website:
Email:
User Name:
Password:
Security Question/Hint
Notes:

Website:
Email:
User Name:
Password:
Security Question/Hint
Notes:

M

Website:
Email:
User Name:
Password:
Security Question/Hint
Notes:

Website:
Email:
User Name:
Password:
Security Question/Hint
Notes:

Website:
Email:
User Name:
Password:
Security Question/Hint
Notes:

M

Website:
Email:
User Name:
Password:
Security Question/Hint
Notes:

Website:
Email:
User Name:
Password:
Security Question/Hint
Notes:

Website:
Email:
User Name:
Password:
Security Question/Hint
Notes:

M

Website:
Email:
User Name:
Password:
Security Question/Hint
Notes:

Website:
Email:
User Name:
Password:
Security Question/Hint
Notes:

Website:
Email:
User Name:
Password:
Security Question/Hint
Notes:

M

Website:
Email:
User Name:
Password:
Security Question/Hint
Notes:

Website:
Email:
User Name:
Password:
Security Question/Hint
Notes:

Website:
Email:
User Name:
Password:
Security Question/Hint
Notes:

Website:
Email:
User Name:
Password:
Security Question/Hint
Notes:

Website:
Email:
User Name:
Password:
Security Question/Hint
Notes:

Website:
Email:
User Name:
Password:
Security Question/Hint
Notes:

N

Website:
Email:
User Name:
Password:
Security Question/Hint
Notes:

Website:
Email:
User Name:
Password:
Security Question/Hint
Notes:

Website:
Email:
User Name:
Password:
Security Question/Hint
Notes:

N

Website:
Email:
User Name:
Password:
Security Question/Hint
Notes:

Website:
Email:
User Name:
Password:
Security Question/Hint
Notes:

Website:
Email:
User Name:
Password:
Security Question/Hint
Notes:

N

| Website: |
| Email: |
| User Name: |
| Password: |
| |
| |
| Security Question/Hint |
| |
| Notes: |
| |

| Website: |
| Email: |
| User Name: |
| Password: |
| |
| |
| Security Question/Hint |
| |
| Notes: |
| |

| Website: |
| Email: |
| User Name: |
| Password: |
| |
| |
| Security Question/Hint |
| |
| Notes: |
| |

O

| Website: |
| Email: |
| User Name: |
| Password: |
| |
| |
| Security Question/Hint |
| |
| Notes: |
| |

| Website: |
| Email: |
| User Name: |
| Password: |
| |
| |
| Security Question/Hint |
| |
| Notes: |
| |

| Website: |
| Email: |
| User Name: |
| Password: |
| |
| |
| Security Question/Hint |
| |
| Notes: |
| |

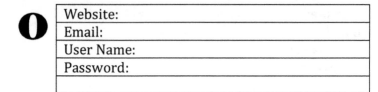

Website:	
Email:	
User Name:	
Password:	
Security Question/Hint	
Notes:	

Website:	
Email:	
User Name:	
Password:	
Security Question/Hint	
Notes:	

Website:	
Email:	
User Name:	
Password:	
Security Question/Hint	
Notes:	

Website:	**O**
Email:	
User Name:	
Password:	
Security Question/Hint	
Notes:	

Website:
Email:
User Name:
Password:
Security Question/Hint
Notes:

Website:
Email:
User Name:
Password:
Security Question/Hint
Notes:

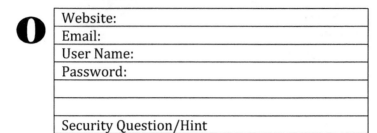

Website:
Email:
User Name:
Password:
Security Question/Hint
Notes:

Website:
Email:
User Name:
Password:
Security Question/Hint
Notes:

Website:
Email:
User Name:
Password:
Security Question/Hint
Notes:

P

Website:
Email:
User Name:
Password:
Security Question/Hint
Notes:

Website:
Email:
User Name:
Password:
Security Question/Hint
Notes:

Website:
Email:
User Name:
Password:
Security Question/Hint
Notes:

P

Website:
Email:
User Name:
Password:
Security Question/Hint
Notes:

Website:
Email:
User Name:
Password:
Security Question/Hint
Notes:

Website:
Email:
User Name:
Password:
Security Question/Hint
Notes:

P

Website:
Email:
User Name:
Password:
Security Question/Hint
Notes:

Website:
Email:
User Name:
Password:
Security Question/Hint
Notes:

Website:
Email:
User Name:
Password:
Security Question/Hint
Notes:

P

Website:
Email:
User Name:
Password:
Security Question/Hint
Notes:

Website:
Email:
User Name:
Password:
Security Question/Hint
Notes:

Website:
Email:
User Name:
Password:
Security Question/Hint
Notes:

Q

Website:
Email:
User Name:
Password:
Security Question/Hint
Notes:

Website:
Email:
User Name:
Password:
Security Question/Hint
Notes:

Website:
Email:
User Name:
Password:
Security Question/Hint
Notes:

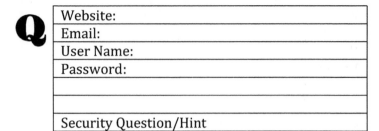

Q

| Website: |
| Email: |
| User Name: |
| Password: |
| |
| |
| Security Question/Hint |
| |
| Notes: |
| |

| Website: |
| Email: |
| User Name: |
| Password: |
| |
| |
| Security Question/Hint |
| |
| Notes: |
| |

| Website: |
| Email: |
| User Name: |
| Password: |
| |
| |
| Security Question/Hint |
| |
| Notes: |
| |

Q

Website:
Email:
User Name:
Password:
Security Question/Hint
Notes:

Website:
Email:
User Name:
Password:
Security Question/Hint
Notes:

Website:
Email:
User Name:
Password:
Security Question/Hint
Notes:

Website:
Email:
User Name:
Password:
Security Question/Hint
Notes:

Website:
Email:
User Name:
Password:
Security Question/Hint
Notes:

Website:
Email:
User Name:
Password:
Security Question/Hint
Notes:

Website:	**R**
Email:	
User Name:	
Password:	
Security Question/Hint	
Notes:	

Website:
Email:
User Name:
Password:
Security Question/Hint
Notes:

Website:
Email:
User Name:
Password:
Security Question/Hint
Notes:

Website:
Email:
User Name:
Password:
Security Question/Hint
Notes:

Website:
Email:
User Name:
Password:
Security Question/Hint
Notes:

Website:
Email:
User Name:
Password:
Security Question/Hint
Notes:

Website:	**R**
Email:	
User Name:	
Password:	
Security Question/Hint	
Notes:	

Website:
Email:
User Name:
Password:
Security Question/Hint
Notes:

Website:
Email:
User Name:
Password:
Security Question/Hint
Notes:

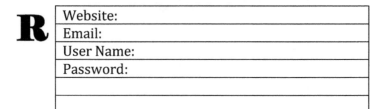

Website:
Email:
User Name:
Password:
Security Question/Hint
Notes:

Website:
Email:
User Name:
Password:
Security Question/Hint
Notes:

Website:
Email:
User Name:
Password:
Security Question/Hint
Notes:

Website:
Email:
User Name:
Password:
Security Question/Hint
Notes:

Website:
Email:
User Name:
Password:
Security Question/Hint
Notes:

Website:
Email:
User Name:
Password:
Security Question/Hint
Notes:

S

Website:
Email:
User Name:
Password:
Security Question/Hint
Notes:

Website:
Email:
User Name:
Password:
Security Question/Hint
Notes:

Website:
Email:
User Name:
Password:
Security Question/Hint
Notes:

S

Website:
Email:
User Name:
Password:
Security Question/Hint
Notes:

Website:
Email:
User Name:
Password:
Security Question/Hint
Notes:

Website:
Email:
User Name:
Password:
Security Question/Hint
Notes:

S

Website:
Email:
User Name:
Password:
Security Question/Hint
Notes:

Website:
Email:
User Name:
Password:
Security Question/Hint
Notes:

Website:
Email:
User Name:
Password:
Security Question/Hint
Notes:

Website:	T
Email:	
User Name:	
Password:	
Security Question/Hint	
Notes:	

Website:
Email:
User Name:
Password:
Security Question/Hint
Notes:

Website:
Email:
User Name:
Password:
Security Question/Hint
Notes:

T

Website:
Email:
User Name:
Password:
Security Question/Hint
Notes:

Website:
Email:
User Name:
Password:
Security Question/Hint
Notes:

Website:
Email:
User Name:
Password:
Security Question/Hint
Notes:

Website:	**T**
Email:	
User Name:	
Password:	
Security Question/Hint	
Notes:	

Website:
Email:
User Name:
Password:
Security Question/Hint
Notes:

Website:
Email:
User Name:
Password:
Security Question/Hint
Notes:

Website:
Email:
User Name:
Password:
Security Question/Hint
Notes:

Website:
Email:
User Name:
Password:
Security Question/Hint
Notes:

Website:
Email:
User Name:
Password:
Security Question/Hint
Notes:

U

Website:
Email:
User Name:
Password:
Security Question/Hint
Notes:

Website:
Email:
User Name:
Password:
Security Question/Hint
Notes:

Website:
Email:
User Name:
Password:
Security Question/Hint
Notes:

U

Website:
Email:
User Name:
Password:
Security Question/Hint
Notes:

Website:
Email:
User Name:
Password:
Security Question/Hint
Notes:

Website:
Email:
User Name:
Password:
Security Question/Hint
Notes:

U

Website:
Email:
User Name:
Password:
Security Question/Hint
Notes:

Website:
Email:
User Name:
Password:
Security Question/Hint
Notes:

Website:
Email:
User Name:
Password:
Security Question/Hint
Notes:

U

Website:
Email:
User Name:
Password:
Security Question/Hint
Notes:

Website:
Email:
User Name:
Password:
Security Question/Hint
Notes:

Website:
Email:
User Name:
Password:
Security Question/Hint
Notes:

V

Website:
Email:
User Name:
Password:
Security Question/Hint
Notes:

Website:
Email:
User Name:
Password:
Security Question/Hint
Notes:

Website:
Email:
User Name:
Password:
Security Question/Hint
Notes:

Website:
Email:
User Name:
Password:
Security Question/Hint
Notes:

Website:
Email:
User Name:
Password:
Security Question/Hint
Notes:

Website:
Email:
User Name:
Password:
Security Question/Hint
Notes:

V

Website:
Email:
User Name:
Password:
Security Question/Hint
Notes:

Website:
Email:
User Name:
Password:
Security Question/Hint
Notes:

Website:
Email:
User Name:
Password:
Security Question/Hint
Notes:

V

Website:
Email:
User Name:
Password:
Security Question/Hint
Notes:

Website:
Email:
User Name:
Password:
Security Question/Hint
Notes:

Website:
Email:
User Name:
Password:
Security Question/Hint
Notes:

Website:	
Email:	**W**
User Name:	
Password:	
Security Question/Hint	
Notes:	

Website:
Email:
User Name:
Password:
Security Question/Hint
Notes:

Website:
Email:
User Name:
Password:
Security Question/Hint
Notes:

Website:
Email:
User Name:
Password:
Security Question/Hint
Notes:

Website:
Email:
User Name:
Password:
Security Question/Hint
Notes:

Website:
Email:
User Name:
Password:
Security Question/Hint
Notes:

Website:
Email:
User Name:
Password:
Security Question/Hint
Notes:

W

Website:
Email:
User Name:
Password:
Security Question/Hint
Notes:

Website:
Email:
User Name:
Password:
Security Question/Hint
Notes:

Website:
Email:
User Name:
Password:
Security Question/Hint
Notes:

Website:
Email:
User Name:
Password:
Security Question/Hint
Notes:

Website:
Email:
User Name:
Password:
Security Question/Hint
Notes:

X

Website:
Email:
User Name:
Password:
Security Question/Hint
Notes:

Website:
Email:
User Name:
Password:
Security Question/Hint
Notes:

Website:
Email:
User Name:
Password:
Security Question/Hint
Notes:

Website:
Email:
User Name:
Password:
Security Question/Hint
Notes:

Website:
Email:
User Name:
Password:
Security Question/Hint
Notes:

Website:
Email:
User Name:
Password:
Security Question/Hint
Notes:

X

Website:	
Email:	
User Name:	
Password:	
Security Question/Hint	
Notes:	

Website:
Email:
User Name:
Password:
Security Question/Hint
Notes:

Website:
Email:
User Name:
Password:
Security Question/Hint
Notes:

Website:
Email:
User Name:
Password:
Security Question/Hint
Notes:

Website:
Email:
User Name:
Password:
Security Question/Hint
Notes:

Website:
Email:
User Name:
Password:
Security Question/Hint
Notes:

Y

Website:
Email:
User Name:
Password:
Security Question/Hint
Notes:

Website:
Email:
User Name:
Password:
Security Question/Hint
Notes:

Website:
Email:
User Name:
Password:
Security Question/Hint
Notes:

Y

| Website: |
| Email: |
| User Name: |
| Password: |
| |
| |
| Security Question/Hint |
| |
| Notes: |
| |

| Website: |
| Email: |
| User Name: |
| Password: |
| |
| |
| Security Question/Hint |
| |
| Notes: |
| |

| Website: |
| Email: |
| User Name: |
| Password: |
| |
| |
| Security Question/Hint |
| |
| Notes: |
| |

Y

Website:	
Email:	
User Name:	
Password:	
Security Question/Hint	
Notes:	

Website:
Email:
User Name:
Password:
Security Question/Hint
Notes:

Website:
Email:
User Name:
Password:
Security Question/Hint
Notes:

Y

Website:
Email:
User Name:
Password:
Security Question/Hint
Notes:

Website:
Email:
User Name:
Password:
Security Question/Hint
Notes:

Website:
Email:
User Name:
Password:
Security Question/Hint
Notes:

| Website: |
| Email: |
| User Name: |
| Password: |
| |
| |
| Security Question/Hint |
| |
| Notes: |
| |

| Website: |
| Email: |
| User Name: |
| Password: |
| |
| |
| Security Question/Hint |
| |
| Notes: |
| |

| Website: |
| Email: |
| User Name: |
| Password: |
| |
| |
| Security Question/Hint |
| |
| Notes: |
| |

Website:
Email:
User Name:
Password:
Security Question/Hint
Notes:

Website:
Email:
User Name:
Password:
Security Question/Hint
Notes:

Website:
Email:
User Name:
Password:
Security Question/Hint
Notes:

Website:
Email:
User Name:
Password:
Security Question/Hint
Notes:

Z

Website:
Email:
User Name:
Password:
Security Question/Hint
Notes:

Website:
Email:
User Name:
Password:
Security Question/Hint
Notes:

Website:
Email:
User Name:
Password:
Security Question/Hint
Notes:

Website:
Email:
User Name:
Password:
Security Question/Hint
Notes:

Website:
Email:
User Name:
Password:
Security Question/Hint
Notes:

≪ NOTES ≫

≪ NOTES ≫

NOTES

≪ NOTES ≫